OUR FAMILY TREE

A History of Our Family

CHARTWELL
BOOKS

Inspiring | Educating | Creating | Entertaining

Brimming with creative inspiration, how-to projects, and useful
information to enrich your everyday life, Quarto Knows is a favorite
destination for those pursuing their interests and passions. Visit our
site and dig deeper with our books into your area of interest:
Quarto Creates, Quarto Cooks, Quarto Homes, Quarto Lives,
Quarto Drives, Quarto Explores, Quarto Gifts, or Quarto Kids.

© 2018 Quarto Publishing Group USA Inc.

This edition published in 2018 by Chartwell Books, an imprint of The Quarto Group,
142 West 36th Street, 4th Floor, New York, NY 10018, USA
T (212) 779-4972 F (212) 779-6058
www.QuartoKnows.com

Chartwell Books titles are also available at discount for retail, wholesale, promotional, and bulk purchase.
For details, contact the Special Sales Manager by email at specialsales@quarto.com or by mail at The Quarto
Group, Attn: Special Sales Manager, 100 Cummings Center Suite 265D,Beverly,MA 01915 USA.

10 9 8 7 6 5 4 3 2

ISBN: 978-07858-3659-9

Cover and book designer: Rachael Cronin
Image credits: Bonney, Devlin, Goldsmith & Hague Family Archives

Printed in China

OUR FAMILY TREE

A History of Our Family

This book is lovingly dedicated to:

_____

This record was compiled by:

_____

_____

Started on:

_____

**A family record is more than names, dates and places. It is about people—
what they did, the why and the how. This book is designed so you can
record forever, in one volume, the history of your family and your ancestors.**

There are sections where you can enter the origins of your family: where your ancestors came from and when, what happened to them, and the things they did. You will also be able to record, perhaps for the first time, stories about members of your family that have been handed down from preceding generations. There are other sections devoted to family photographs traditions and such memorable events as weddings and reunions. And there is a most important "how to" section that will help you trace your family's history: where to write and obtain records, what information to include in such inquiries,

and what institutions are available to you for further assistance (such as libraries, and book-stores that specialize in genealogy information).

From the birth of a great-great-grandparent to the birth of the newest baby in your family, his book provides a wonderful opportunity to gather together in one place all the interesting and unusual aspects of your family's history. When complete, it will be a storehouse of treasured information, achievements and memories—a permanent record of your family which is unique and not like any other.

Our Family

This certifies that

_____

and

_____

Were United in Holy Matrimony

Place of Ceremony _____

_____

City _____ State _____

Month _____ Day _____ Year _____

Married by _____

_____

Husband's Genealogy

Husband's Full Name _____

_____

Birth Date _____

Birth Place _____

Father's Full Name _____

_____

Mother's Full Name _____

_____

Brothers and Sisters _____

_____

_____

_____

_____

_____

_____

_____

Wife's Genealogy

Wife's Full Name _____

_____

Birth Date _____

Birth Place _____

Father's Full Name _____

_____

Mother's Full Name _____

_____

Brothers and Sisters _____

_____

_____

_____

_____

_____

_____

_____

Our Children

Full Name	Place of Birth	Date of Birth

Our Grandchildren
& Descendants

_____

_____

_____

_____

_____

_____

_____

_____

_____

_____

_____

_____

_____

_____

Our Family Tree

Husband's Full Name _____

_____

Wife's Full Name _____

_____

Date of Marriage _____

Place of Marriage _____

Our Children _____

_____

_____

_____

_____

Who we are & where we came from

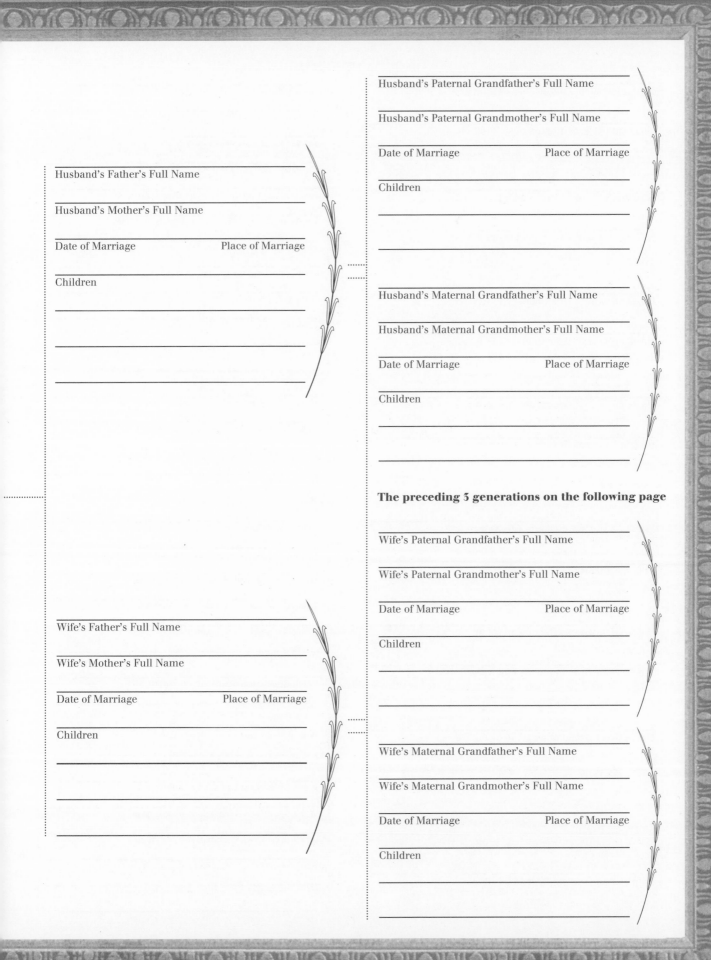

Husband's Paternal Grandfather's Full Name

Husband's Paternal Grandmother's Full Name

Date of Marriage   Place of Marriage

Children

Husband's Father's Full Name

Husband's Mother's Full Name

Date of Marriage   Place of Marriage

Children

Husband's Maternal Grandfather's Full Name

Husband's Maternal Grandmother's Full Name

Date of Marriage   Place of Marriage

Children

The preceding 3 generations on the following page

Wife's Paternal Grandfather's Full Name

Wife's Paternal Grandmother's Full Name

Date of Marriage   Place of Marriage

Children

Wife's Father's Full Name

Wife's Mother's Full Name

Date of Marriage   Place of Marriage

Children

Wife's Maternal Grandfather's Full Name

Wife's Maternal Grandmother's Full Name

Date of Marriage   Place of Marriage

Children

Husband's Great-Grandfather's Full Name

Husband's Great-Grandmother's Full Name

Husband's Great-Grandfather's Full Name

Husband's Great-Grandmother's Full Name

Husband's Great-Grandfather's Full Name

Husband's Great-Grandmother's Full Name

Husband's Great-Grandfather's Full Name

Husband's Great-Grandmother's Full Name

Husband's Great-Great-Grandfather's Full Name

Husband's Great-Great-Grandmother's Full Name

Husband's Great-Great-Grandfather's Full Name

Husband's Great-Great-Grandmother's Full Name

Husband's Great-Great-Grandfather's Full Name

Husband's Great-Great-Grandmother's Full Name

Husband's Great-Great-Grandfather's Full Name

Husband's Great-Great-Grandmother's Full Name

Husband's Great-Great-Grandfather's Full Name

Husband's Great-Great-Grandmother's Full Name

Husband's Great-Great-Grandfather's Full Name

Husband's Great-Great-Grandmother's Full Name

Husband's Great-Great-Grandfather's Full Name

Husband's Great-Great-Grandmother's Full Name

Husband's Great-Great-Grandfather's Full Name

Husband's Great-Great-Grandmother's Full Name

Wife's Great-Grandfather's Full Name

Wife's Great-Grandmother's Full Name

Wife's Great-Grandfather's Full Name

Wife's Great-Grandmother's Full Name

Wife's Great-Grandfather's Full Name

Wife's Great-Grandmother's Full Name

Wife's Great-Grandfather's Full Name

Wife's Great-Grandmother's Full Name

Wife's Great-Great-Grandfather's Full Name

Wife's Great-Great-Grandmother's Full Name

Wife's Great-Great-Grandfather's Full Name

Wife's Great-Great-Grandmother's Full Name

Wife's Great-Great-Grandfather's Full Name

Wife's Great-Great-Grandmother's Full Name

Wife's Great-Great-Grandfather's Full Name

Wife's Great-Great-Grandmother's Full Name

Wife's Great-Great-Grandfather's Full Name

Wife's Great-Great-Grandmother's Full Name

Wife's Great-Great-Grandfather's Full Name

Wife's Great-Great-Grandmother's Full Name

Wife's Great-Great-Grandfather's Full Name

Wife's Great-Great-Grandmother's Full Name

Wife's Great-Great-Grandfather's Full Name

Wife's Great-Great-Grandmother's Full Name

Great-Great-Great-Grandparents

Mr. & Mrs. _____ NEE _____

Mr. & Mrs. _____ NEE _____

Mr. & Mrs. _____ NEE _____

Mr. & Mrs. _____ NEE _____

Mr. & Mrs. _____ NEE _____

Mr. & Mrs. _____ NEE _____

Mr. & Mrs. _____ NEE _____

Mr. & Mrs. _____ NEE _____

Mr. & Mrs. _____ NEE _____

Mr. & Mrs. _____ NEE _____

Mr. & Mrs. _____ NEE _____

Mr. & Mrs. _____ NEE _____

Mr. & Mrs. _____ NEE _____

Mr. & Mrs. _____ NEE _____

Mr. & Mrs. _____ NEE _____

Mr. & Mrs. _____ NEE _____

Mr. & Mrs. _____ NEE _____

Mr. & Mrs. _____ NEE _____

Mr. & Mrs. _____ NEE _____

Mr. & Mrs. _____ NEE _____

Mr. & Mrs. _____ NEE _____

Mr. & Mrs. _____ NEE _____

Mr. & Mrs. _____ NEE _____

Mr. & Mrs. _____ NEE _____

Mr. & Mrs. _____ NEE _____

Mr. & Mrs. _____ NEE _____

Mr. & Mrs. _____ NEE _____

Mr. & Mrs. _____ NEE _____

Mr. & Mrs. _____ NEE _____

Mr. & Mrs. _____ NEE _____

Mr. & Mrs. _____ NEE _____

Mr. & Mrs. _____ NEE _____

The generations preceding the one in the column on the left would have been born about 1800 and of course would be double the number.

Each generation going back in time will be twice the number.

NEE represents Wife's Maiden Name

Husband's Ancestral Chart

Husband's Full Name _____

Date of Birth _____

Place of Birth _____

Date of Marriage _____

Place of Marriage _____

Date of Death _____

Place of Burial _____

Occupation _____

_____

Special Interests _____

_____

Father's Full Name

Date of Birth   Place of Birth

Date of Marriage   Place of Marriage

Date of Death   Place of Burial

Occupation

Special Interests

Mother's Full Name

Date of Birth   Place of Birth

Date of Marriage   Place of Marriage

Date of Death   Place of Burial

Occupation

Special Interests

Father's Full Name

Date of Birth   Place of Birth

Date of Marriage   Place of Marriage

Date of Death   Place of Burial

Occupation

Special Interests

Mother's Full Name

Date of Birth   Place of Birth

Date of Marriage   Place of Marriage

Date of Death   Place of Burial

Occupation

Special Interests

The preceding 3 generations on the following page

Father's Full Name

Date of Birth   Place of Birth

Date of Marriage   Place of Marriage

Date of Death   Place of Burial

Occupation

Special Interests

Father's Full Name

Date of Birth   Place of Birth

Date of Marriage   Place of Marriage

Date of Death   Place of Burial

Occupation

Special Interests

Great-Grandfather's Full Name
_____

Date of Birth   Place of Birth
_____

Occupation
_____

Great-Grandmother's Full Name
_____

Date of Birth   Place of Birth
_____

Occupation
_____

Great-Grandfather's Full Name
_____

Date of Birth   Place of Birth
_____

Occupation
_____

Great-Grandmother's Full Name
_____

Date of Birth   Place of Birth
_____

Occupation
_____

Great-Grandfather's Full Name
_____

Date of Birth   Place of Birth
_____

Occupation
_____

Great-Grandmother's Full Name
_____

Date of Birth   Place of Birth
_____

Occupation
_____

Great-Grandfather's Full Name
_____

Date of Birth   Place of Birth
_____

Occupation
_____

Great-Grandmother's Full Name
_____

Date of Birth   Place of Birth
_____

Occupation
_____

Great-Grandfather's Full Name
_____

Great-Grandmother's Full Name
_____

Great-Grandfather's Full Name
_____

Great-Grandmother's Full Name
_____

Great-Grandfather's Full Name
_____

Great-Grandmother's Full Name
_____

Great-Grandfather's Full Name
_____

Great-Grandmother's Full Name
_____

Great-Grandfather's Full Name
_____

Great-Grandmother's Full Name
_____

Great-Grandfather's Full Name
_____

Great-Grandmother's Full Name
_____

Great-Grandfather's Full Name
_____

Great-Grandmother's Full Name
_____

Great-Grandfather's Full Name
_____

Great-Grandmother's Full Name
_____

Great-Great-Great-Grandparents

Mr. & Mrs. _____ NEE _____

Mr. & Mrs. _____ NEE _____

Mr. & Mrs. _____ NEE _____

Mr. & Mrs. _____ NEE _____

Mr. & Mrs. _____ NEE _____

Mr. & Mrs. _____ NEE _____

Mr. & Mrs. _____ NEE _____

Mr. & Mrs. _____ NEE _____

Mr. & Mrs. _____ NEE _____

Mr. & Mrs. _____ NEE _____

Mr. & Mrs. _____ NEE _____

Mr. & Mrs. _____ NEE _____

Mr. & Mrs. _____ NEE _____

Mr. & Mrs. _____ NEE _____

Mr. & Mrs. _____ NEE _____

Mr. & Mrs. _____ NEE _____

Mr. & Mrs. _____ NEE _____

Mr. & Mrs. _____ NEE _____

Mr. & Mrs. _____ NEE _____

Mr. & Mrs. _____ NEE _____

Mr. & Mrs. _____ NEE _____

Mr. & Mrs. _____ NEE _____

Mr. & Mrs. _____ NEE _____

Mr. & Mrs. _____ NEE _____

Mr. & Mrs. _____ NEE _____

Mr. & Mrs. _____ NEE _____

Mr. & Mrs. _____ NEE _____

Mr. & Mrs. _____ NEE _____

Mr. & Mrs. _____ NEE _____

Mr. & Mrs. _____ NEE _____

Mr. & Mrs. _____ NEE _____

Mr. & Mrs. _____ NEE _____

For a variety of reasons, families have altered the spelling of the last name or changed it completely.

So in looking back and trying to get information from the county city or town overseas that your family came from, make sure you include as much data as you can before writing abroad.

NEE represents Wife's Maiden Name

Husband's Family

On this and the next page, fill in all vital statistics on the Husband,
his Brothers and Sisters, and their Children (Nieces and Nephews).

Husband, his Brothers and Sisters, and their Children

Name _____ Born _____ Died _____ Spouse _____

    Children _____

_____

Name _____ Born _____ Died _____ Spouse _____

    Children _____

_____

Name _____ Born _____ Died _____ Spouse _____

    Children _____

_____

Name _____ Born _____ Died _____ Spouse _____

    Children _____

_____

Name _____ Born _____ Died _____ Spouse _____

    Children _____

_____

Name _____ Born _____ Died _____ Spouse _____

    Children _____

_____

Legal Guardians

Fill in the names of Legal Guardians for any child where applicable,
including dates, places and any information you consider appropriate.

_____

_____

_____

_____

_____

_____

_____

_____

_____

_____

_____

_____

_____

_____

_____

_____

Husband's Parent's Family

On this and the next page, fill in all vital statistics on the Husband's Parents, their Brothers and Sisters (Aunts and Uncles), and their Children (Cousins).

Husband's Father, his Brothers and Sisters, and their Children

Name _____ Born _____ Died _____ Spouse _____

    Children _____

_____

Name _____ Born _____ Died _____ Spouse _____

    Children _____

_____

Name _____ Born _____ Died _____ Spouse _____

    Children _____

_____

Name _____ Born _____ Died _____ Spouse _____

    Children _____

_____

Name _____ Born _____ Died _____ Spouse _____

    Children _____

_____

Name _____ Born _____ Died _____ Spouse _____

    Children _____

_____

Legal Guardians

Fill in the names of Legal Guardians for any child where applicable,
including dates, places and any information you consider appropriate.

_____

_____

_____

_____

_____

_____

_____

_____

_____

_____

_____

_____

_____

_____

_____

_____

_____

_____

Husband's Parent's Family

CONTINUED

Husband's Mother, her Brothers and Sisters, and their Children

Name _____ Born _____ Died _____ Spouse _____

    Children _____

_____

Name _____ Born _____ Died _____ Spouse _____

    Children _____

_____

Name _____ Born _____ Died _____ Spouse _____

    Children _____

_____

Name _____ Born _____ Died _____ Spouse _____

    Children _____

_____

Name _____ Born _____ Died _____ Spouse _____

    Children _____

_____

Name _____ Born _____ Died _____ Spouse _____

    Children _____

_____

Legal Guardians

Fill in the names of Legal Guardians for any child where applicable,
including dates, places and any information you consider appropriate.

_____

_____

_____

_____

_____

_____

_____

_____

_____

_____

_____

_____

_____

_____

_____

_____

Husband's Grandparents

Father's Side

Grandfather, his Brothers and Sisters, and their Children

Name _____ Born _____ Died _____ Spouse _____

    Children _____

_____

Name _____ Born _____ Died _____ Spouse _____

    Children _____

_____

Name _____ Born _____ Died _____ Spouse _____

    Children _____

_____

Name _____ Born _____ Died _____ Spouse _____

    Children _____

_____

Name _____ Born _____ Died _____ Spouse _____

    Children _____

_____

Name _____ Born _____ Died _____ Spouse _____

    Children _____

_____

Legal Guardians

Fill in the names of Legal Guardians for any child where applicable,
including dates, places and any information you consider appropriate.

Husband's Grandparents

Father's Side

Grandmother, her Brothers and Sisters, and their Children

Name _____ Born _____ Died _____ Spouse _____

    Children _____

_____

Name _____ Born _____ Died _____ Spouse _____

    Children _____

_____

Name _____ Born _____ Died _____ Spouse _____

    Children _____

_____

Name _____ Born _____ Died _____ Spouse _____

    Children _____

_____

Name _____ Born _____ Died _____ Spouse _____

    Children _____

_____

Name _____ Born _____ Died _____ Spouse _____

    Children _____

_____

Legal Guardians

Fill in the names of Legal Guardians for any child where applicable,
including dates, places and any information you consider appropriate.

_____

_____

_____

_____

_____

_____

_____

_____

_____

_____

_____

_____

_____

_____

_____

Husband's Grandparents

Mother's Side

Grandfather, his Brothers and Sisters, and their Children

Name _____ Born _____ Died _____ Spouse _____

    Children _____

_____

Name _____ Born _____ Died _____ Spouse _____

    Children _____

_____

Name _____ Born _____ Died _____ Spouse _____

    Children _____

_____

Name _____ Born _____ Died _____ Spouse _____

    Children _____

_____

Name _____ Born _____ Died _____ Spouse _____

    Children _____

_____

Name _____ Born _____ Died _____ Spouse _____

    Children _____

_____

Legal Guardians

Fill in the names of Legal Guardians for any child where applicable,
including dates, places and any information you consider appropriate.

_____

_____

_____

_____

_____

_____

_____

_____

_____

_____

_____

_____

_____

_____

Husband's Grandparents

Mother's Side

Grandmother, her Brothers and Sisters, and their Children

Name _____ Born _____ Died _____ Spouse _____

      Children _____

_____

Name _____ Born _____ Died _____ Spouse _____

      Children _____

_____

Name _____ Born _____ Died _____ Spouse _____

      Children _____

_____

Name _____ Born _____ Died _____ Spouse _____

      Children _____

_____

Name _____ Born _____ Died _____ Spouse _____

      Children _____

_____

Name _____ Born _____ Died _____ Spouse _____

      Children _____

_____

Legal Guardians

Fill in the names of Legal Guardians for any child where applicable,
including dates, places and any information you consider appropriate.

_____

_____

_____

_____

_____

_____

_____

_____

_____

_____

_____

_____

_____

_____

_____

_____

Husband's
Great Grandparents

Name _____ Born _____ Died _____ Spouse _____

Children _____

_____

Name _____ Born _____ Died _____ Spouse _____

Children _____

_____

Name _____ Born _____ Died _____ Spouse _____

Children _____

_____

Name _____ Born _____ Died _____ Spouse _____

Children _____

_____

Name _____ Born _____ Died _____ Spouse _____

Children _____

_____

Name _____ Born _____ Died _____ Spouse _____

Children _____

_____

Legal Guardians

Fill in the names of Legal Guardians for any child where applicable,
including dates, places and any information you consider appropriate.

Wife's Ancestral Chart

Wife's Full Name _____

Date of Birth _____

Place of Birth _____

Date of Marriage _____

Place of Marriage _____

Date of Death _____

Place of Burial _____

Occupation _____

_____

Special Interests _____

_____

Father's Full Name

Date of Birth   Place of Birth

Date of Marriage   Place of Marriage

Date of Death   Place of Burial

Occupation

Special Interests

Father's Full Name

Date of Birth   Place of Birth

Date of Marriage   Place of Marriage

Date of Death   Place of Burial

Occupation

Special Interests

Mother's Full Name

Date of Birth   Place of Birth

Date of Marriage   Place of Marriage

Date of Death   Place of Burial

Occupation

Special Interests

The preceding 3 generations on the following page

Father's Full Name

Date of Birth   Place of Birth

Date of Marriage   Place of Marriage

Date of Death   Place of Burial

Occupation

Special Interests

Mother's Full Name

Date of Birth   Place of Birth

Date of Marriage   Place of Marriage

Date of Death   Place of Burial

Occupation

Special Interests

Father's Full Name

Date of Birth   Place of Birth

Date of Marriage   Place of Marriage

Date of Death   Place of Burial

Occupation

Special Interests

Great-Grandfather's Full Name

Date of Birth   Place of Birth

Occupation

Great-Grandmother's Full Name

Date of Birth   Place of Birth

Occupation

Great-Grandfather's Full Name

Date of Birth   Place of Birth

Occupation

Great-Grandmother's Full Name

Date of Birth   Place of Birth

Occupation

Great-Grandfather's Full Name

Date of Birth   Place of Birth

Occupation

Great-Grandmother's Full Name

Date of Birth   Place of Birth

Occupation

Great-Grandfather's Full Name

Date of Birth   Place of Birth

Occupation

Great-Grandmother's Full Name

Date of Birth   Place of Birth

Occupation

Great-Grandfather's Full Name

Great-Grandmother's Full Name

Great-Grandfather's Full Name

Great-Grandmother's Full Name

Great-Grandfather's Full Name

Great-Grandmother's Full Name

Great-Grandfather's Full Name

Great-Grandmother's Full Name

Great-Grandfather's Full Name

Great-Grandmother's Full Name

Great-Grandfather's Full Name

Great-Grandmother's Full Name

Great-Grandfather's Full Name

Great-Grandmother's Full Name

Great-Grandfather's Full Name

Great-Grandmother's Full Name

Great-Great-Great-Grandparents

Mr. & Mrs. _____ NEE _____

Mr. & Mrs. _____ NEE _____

Mr. & Mrs. _____ NEE _____

Mr. & Mrs. _____ NEE _____

Mr. & Mrs. _____ NEE _____

Mr. & Mrs. _____ NEE _____

Mr. & Mrs. _____ NEE _____

Mr. & Mrs. _____ NEE _____

Mr. & Mrs. _____ NEE _____

Mr. & Mrs. _____ NEE _____

Mr. & Mrs. _____ NEE _____

Mr. & Mrs. _____ NEE _____

Mr. & Mrs. _____ NEE _____

Mr. & Mrs. _____ NEE _____

Mr. & Mrs. _____ NEE _____

Mr. & Mrs. _____ NEE _____

Mr. & Mrs. _____ NEE _____

Mr. & Mrs. _____ NEE _____

Mr. & Mrs. _____ NEE _____

Mr. & Mrs. _____ NEE _____

If your ancestors
landed here in 1600
and you are under 30,
you would be the
14th of 15th
generation and be
descended from over
16,000 people.

Mr. & Mrs. _____ NEE _____

Mr. & Mrs. _____ NEE _____

Mr. & Mrs. _____ NEE _____

Mr. & Mrs. _____ NEE _____

Mr. & Mrs. _____ NEE _____

Mr. & Mrs. _____ NEE _____

Mr. & Mrs. _____ NEE _____

Mr. & Mrs. _____ NEE _____

Mr. & Mrs. _____ NEE _____

Mr. & Mrs. _____ NEE _____

Mr. & Mrs. _____ NEE _____

NEE represents Wife's Maiden Name

Mr. & Mrs. _____ NEE _____

Wife's Family

On this and the next page, fill in all vital statistics on the Wife,
her Brothers and Sisters, and their Children (Nieces and Nephews).

Wife, her Brothers and Sisters, and their Children

Name _____ Born _____ Died _____ Spouse _____

   Children _____

   _____

Name _____ Born _____ Died _____ Spouse _____

   Children _____

   _____

Name _____ Born _____ Died _____ Spouse _____

   Children _____

   _____

Name _____ Born _____ Died _____ Spouse _____

   Children _____

   _____

Name _____ Born _____ Died _____ Spouse _____

   Children _____

   _____

Name _____ Born _____ Died _____ Spouse _____

   Children _____

   _____

Legal Guardians

Fill in the names of Legal Guardians for any child where applicable,
including dates, places and any information you consider appropriate.

_____

_____

_____

_____

_____

_____

_____

_____

_____

_____

_____

_____

_____

_____

_____

_____

Wife's Parents Family

On this and the next page, fill in all vital statistics on the Wife's Parents,
their Brothers and Sisters (Aunts and Uncles), and their Children (Cousins).

Wife's Father, his Brothers and Sisters, and their Children

Name   Born   Died   Spouse

     Children

Name   Born   Died   Spouse

     Children

Name   Born   Died   Spouse

     Children

Name   Born   Died   Spouse

     Children

Name   Born   Died   Spouse

     Children

Name   Born   Died   Spouse

     Children

Legal Guardians

Fill in the names of Legal Guardians for any child where applicable,
including dates, places and any information you consider appropriate.

Wife's Parents Family

CONTINUED

Wife's Mother, her Brothers and Sisters, and their Children

Name _____ Born _____ Died _____ Spouse _____

    Children _____

_____

Name _____ Born _____ Died _____ Spouse _____

    Children _____

_____

Name _____ Born _____ Died _____ Spouse _____

    Children _____

_____

Name _____ Born _____ Died _____ Spouse _____

    Children _____

_____

Name _____ Born _____ Died _____ Spouse _____

    Children _____

_____

Name _____ Born _____ Died _____ Spouse _____

    Children _____

_____

Legal Guardians

Fill in the names of Legal Guardians for any child where applicable,
including dates, places and any information you consider appropriate.

_____

_____

_____

_____

_____

_____

_____

_____

_____

_____

_____

_____

_____

_____

_____

Wife's Grandparents

Father's Side

Grandfather, her Brothers and Sisters, and their Children

Name _____ Born _____ Died _____ Spouse _____

    Children _____

_____

Name _____ Born _____ Died _____ Spouse _____

    Children _____

_____

Name _____ Born _____ Died _____ Spouse _____

    Children _____

_____

Name _____ Born _____ Died _____ Spouse _____

    Children _____

_____

Name _____ Born _____ Died _____ Spouse _____

    Children _____

_____

Name _____ Born _____ Died _____ Spouse _____

    Children _____

_____

Legal Guardians

Fill in the names of Legal Guardians for any child where applicable,
including dates, places and any information you consider appropriate.

_____

_____

_____

_____

_____

_____

_____

_____

_____

_____

_____

_____

_____

_____

_____

_____

_____

Wife's Grandparents

Father's Side

Grandmother, her Brothers and Sisters, and their Children

Name _____ Born _____ Died _____ Spouse _____

    Children _____

_____

Name _____ Born _____ Died _____ Spouse _____

    Children _____

_____

Name _____ Born _____ Died _____ Spouse _____

    Children _____

_____

Name _____ Born _____ Died _____ Spouse _____

    Children _____

_____

Name _____ Born _____ Died _____ Spouse _____

    Children _____

_____

Name _____ Born _____ Died _____ Spouse _____

    Children _____

_____

Legal Guardians

Fill in the names of Legal Guardians for any child where applicable,
including dates, places and any information you consider appropriate.

Wife's Grandparents

Mother's Side

Grandfather, his Brothers and Sisters, and their Children

Name _____ Born _____ Died _____ Spouse _____

    Children _____

_____

Name _____ Born _____ Died _____ Spouse _____

    Children _____

_____

Name _____ Born _____ Died _____ Spouse _____

    Children _____

_____

Name _____ Born _____ Died _____ Spouse _____

    Children _____

_____

Name _____ Born _____ Died _____ Spouse _____

    Children _____

_____

Name _____ Born _____ Died _____ Spouse _____

    Children _____

_____

Legal Guardians

Fill in the names of Legal Guardians for any child where applicable,
including dates, places and any information you consider appropriate.

_____

_____

_____

_____

_____

_____

_____

_____

_____

_____

_____

_____

_____

_____

_____

_____

_____

Wife's Grandparents

Mother's Side

Grandmother, her Brothers and Sisters, and their Children

Name _____ Born _____ Died _____ Spouse _____

　　　Children _____

_____

Name _____ Born _____ Died _____ Spouse _____

　　　Children _____

_____

Name _____ Born _____ Died _____ Spouse _____

　　　Children _____

_____

Name _____ Born _____ Died _____ Spouse _____

　　　Children _____

_____

Name _____ Born _____ Died _____ Spouse _____

　　　Children _____

_____

Name _____ Born _____ Died _____ Spouse _____

　　　Children _____

_____

Legal Guardians

Fill in the names of Legal Guardians for any child where applicable, including dates, places and any information you consider appropriate.

_____

_____

_____

_____

_____

_____

_____

_____

_____

_____

_____

_____

_____

_____

_____

_____

_____

Wife's
Great Grandparents

Name _____ Born _____ Died _____ Spouse _____

　　　Children _____

　　　_____

Name _____ Born _____ Died _____ Spouse _____

　　　Children _____

　　　_____

Name _____ Born _____ Died _____ Spouse _____

　　　Children _____

　　　_____

Name _____ Born _____ Died _____ Spouse _____

　　　Children _____

　　　_____

Name _____ Born _____ Died _____ Spouse _____

　　　Children _____

　　　_____

Name _____ Born _____ Died _____ Spouse _____

　　　Children _____

　　　_____

Legal Guardians

Fill in the names of Legal Guardians for any child where applicable, including dates, places and any information you consider appropriate.

Citizenship Record

Name _____ Emigrated from _____ To _____ Date _____

_____

_____

_____

_____

Name _____ Emigrated from _____ To _____ Date _____

_____

_____

_____

_____

Name _____ Emigrated from _____ To _____ Date _____

_____

_____

_____

_____

Name _____ Emigrated from _____ To _____ Date _____

_____

_____

_____

_____

In the space below fill in the countries your family came from along with any other information about that place you have or can get. Also, put in when the family emigrated, where they landed and how your branch settled where it is now.

Name   Emigrated from   To   Date

_____

_____

_____

_____

Name   Emigrated from   To   Date

_____

_____

_____

_____

Name   Emigrated from   To   Date

_____

_____

_____

_____

Name   Emigrated from   To   Date

_____

_____

_____

_____

Citizenship Record

CONTINUED

Name	Emigrated from	To	Date

Name	Emigrated from	To	Date

Name	Emigrated from	To	Date

Name	Emigrated from	To	Date

Name _____ Emigrated from _____ To _____ Date _____

_____

_____

_____

_____

Name _____ Emigrated from _____ To _____ Date _____

_____

_____

_____

_____

Name _____ Emigrated from _____ To _____ Date _____

_____

_____

_____

_____

Name _____ Emigrated from _____ To _____ Date _____

_____

_____

_____

_____

Name _____ Emigrated from _____ To _____ Date _____

_____

_____

_____

_____

Weddings

Names   Date   Location

Names   Date   Location

Names   Date   Location

Names   Date   Location

Names   Date   Location

Names   Date   Location

_____

_____

_____

Names   Date   Location

_____

_____

_____

Names   Date   Location

_____

_____

_____

Names   Date   Location

_____

_____

_____

Names   Date   Location

_____

_____

Notes

_____

_____

_____

Weddings

CONTINUED

Names   Date   Location

Names   Date   Location

Names   Date   Location

Names   Date   Location

Names   Date   Location

Names _____ Date _____ Location _____
_____
_____
_____

Names _____ Date _____ Location _____
_____
_____

Names _____ Date _____ Location _____
_____
_____
_____

Names _____ Date _____ Location _____
_____
_____
_____

Names _____ Date _____ Location _____
_____
_____
_____

Notes _____
_____
_____
_____

Religious Occasions

Name _____

Ceremony or Occasion _____

Godparents or Sponsor _____

Date and Location _____

Name _____

Ceremony or Occasion _____

Godparents or Sponsor _____

Date and Location _____

Name _____

Ceremony or Occasion _____

Godparents or Sponsor _____

Date and Location _____

Name _____

Ceremony or Occasion _____

Godparents or Sponsor _____

Date and Location _____

Name _____

Ceremony or Occasion _____

Godparents or Sponsor _____

Date and Location _____

Name _____

Ceremony or Occasion _____

Godparents or Sponsor _____

Date and Location _____

Name _____

Ceremony or Occasion _____

Godparents or Sponsor _____

Date and Location _____

Name _____

Ceremony or Occasion _____

Godparents or Sponsor _____

Date and Location _____

Notes _____

_____

_____

_____

Religious Occasions

CONTINUED

Name

Ceremony or Occasion

Godparents or Sponsor

Date and Location

Name

Ceremony or Occasion

Godparents or Sponsor

Date and Location

Name

Ceremony or Occasion

Godparents or Sponsor

Date and Location

Name

Ceremony or Occasion

Godparents or Sponsor

Date and Location

Our Places of Worship

In Memoriam

Here you may record names of those who have died about whom you have special memories.
You may write stories you have heard or your own personal thoughts.

_____

_____

_____

_____

_____

_____

_____

_____

_____

_____

_____

_____

_____

_____

In Memoriam

CONTINUED

Our Homes

Street _____

City _____ State _____

Date of Purchase _____ Resided from _____ to _____

_____

_____

_____

_____

_____

_____

Street _____

City _____ State _____

Date of Purchase _____ Resided from _____ to _____

_____

_____

_____

_____

_____

_____

_____

Street _____

City _____ State _____

Date of Purchase _____ Resided from _____ to _____

_____

_____

_____

_____

_____

Street _____

City _____ State _____

Date of Purchase _____ Resided from _____ to _____

_____

_____

_____

_____

_____

Street _____

City _____ State _____

Date of Purchase _____ Resided from _____ to _____

_____

_____

_____

_____

_____

Our Homes

CONTINUED

Street _____

City _____ State _____

Date of Purchase _____ Resided from _____ to _____

_____

_____

_____

_____

_____

_____

_____

Street _____

City _____ State _____

Date of Purchase _____ Resided from _____ to _____

_____

_____

_____

_____

_____

_____

Our Ancestors' Homes

_____
_____
_____
_____
_____
_____
_____
_____
_____
_____
_____
_____
_____
_____
_____
_____
_____
_____
_____
_____
_____
_____
_____

Schools & Graduations

Name _____

School, College or University _____

Dates of Attendance _____ Certificate or Degree _____

Name _____

School, College or University _____

Dates of Attendance _____ Certificate or Degree _____

Name _____

School, College or University _____

Dates of Attendance _____ Certificate or Degree _____

Name _____

School, College or University _____

Dates of Attendance _____ Certificate or Degree _____

Name _____

School, College or University _____

Dates of Attendance _____ Certificate or Degree _____

Schools & Graduations

Important School Achievements —
Fine Arts, Athletics, and Other Awards

Name

Achievement

School   Date

Name

Achievement

School   Date

Name

Achievement

School   Date

Name

Achievement

School   Date

Name

Achievement

School   Date

Clubs & Organizations

Fill in the names of family members and their clubs and organizations, including offices held and any other interesting information about the person or organization.

Name _____

Organization _____

Activity, Award, Office Held _____ Date _____

_____

Name _____

Organization _____

Activity, Award, Office Held _____ Date _____

_____

Name _____

Organization _____

Activity, Award, Office Held _____ Date _____

_____

Name _____

Organization _____

Activity, Award, Office Held _____ Date _____

Companies
Where We Worked

Record here employment histories and businesses started by
any member of your family, including when and where a business
was begun and its success or failure and why.

Family Member _____

Company _____

Dates of Service _____ Position _____

Family Member _____

Company _____

Dates of Service _____ Position _____

Family Member _____

Company _____

Dates of Service _____ Position _____

Family Member _____

Company _____

Dates of Service _____ Position _____

Family Member _____

Company _____

Dates of Service _____ Position _____

Family Member _____

Company _____

Dates of Service _____ Position _____

Family Member _____

Company _____

Dates of Service _____ Position _____

Family Member _____

Company _____

Dates of Service _____ Position _____

Family Member _____

Company _____

Dates of Service _____ Position _____

Family Member _____

Company _____

Dates of Service _____ Position _____

Family Member _____

Company _____

Dates of Service _____ Position _____

Family Member _____

Company _____

Dates of Service _____ Position _____

Companies
Where We Worked

CONTINUED

Family Member _____

Company _____

Dates of Service _____ Position _____

Family Member _____

Company _____

Dates of Service _____ Position _____

Family Member _____

Company _____

Dates of Service _____ Position _____

Family Member _____

Company _____

Dates of Service _____ Position _____

Family Member _____

Company _____

Dates of Service _____ Position _____

Family Member _____

Company _____

Dates of Service _____ Position _____

Family Member _____

Company _____

Dates of Service _____ Position _____

Family Member _____

Company _____

Dates of Service _____ Position _____

Family Member _____

Company _____

Dates of Service _____ Position _____

Family Member _____

Company _____

Dates of Service _____ Position _____

Family Member _____

Company _____

Dates of Service _____ Position _____

Family Member _____

Company _____

Dates of Service _____ Position _____

Family Member _____

Company _____

Dates of Service _____ Position _____

Military Service Records

Name _____ Service Number _____ Job Classification _____

Enlisted or Inducted _____ Month _____ Day _____ Year _____ At Age _____

Branch of Service _____ Grade _____

Training Camps _____ Service Schools Attended _____

_____

Division _____ Regiment _____ Department or Ship _____ Dates _____

Company _____ Transferred _____

Promotion and Dates _____

_____

_____

Overseas Service _____ Departure Date _____ Port _____ Return Date _____ Port _____

_____

_____

Battles, Engagements, Skirmishes, Expeditions _____ Commanding Officers _____ Citations _____

_____

_____

Wounds Received in Service; Sickness or Hospitalization _____

_____

_____

Important Leaves or Furloughs _____

Discharged at or Separation _____

Name _____ Service Number _____ Job Classification _____

Enlisted or Inducted _____ Month _____ Day _____ Year _____ At Age _____

Branch of Service _____ Grade _____

Training Camps _____ Service Schools Attended _____

_____

Division _____ Regiment _____ Department or Ship _____ Dates _____

Company _____ Transferred _____

Promotion and Dates _____

_____

_____

Overseas Service _____ Departure Date _____ Port _____ Return Date _____ Port _____

_____

_____

Battles, Engagements, Skirmishes, Expeditions _____ Commanding Officers _____ Citations _____

_____

_____

Wounds Received in Service; Sickness or Hospitalization _____

_____

_____

Important Leaves or Furloughs _____

Discharged at or Separation _____

Notes: _____

_____

_____

Military Service Records

Name _____ Service Number _____ Job Classification _____

Enlisted or Inducted _____ Month _____ Day _____ Year _____ At Age _____

Branch of Service _____ Grade _____

Training Camps _____ Service Schools Attended _____

_____

Division _____ Regiment _____ Department or Ship _____ Dates _____

Company _____ Transferred _____

Promotion and Dates _____

_____

_____

Overseas Service _____ Departure Date _____ Port _____ Return Date _____ Port _____

_____

_____

Battles, Engagements, Skirmishes, Expeditions _____ Commanding Officers _____ Citations _____

_____

_____

Wounds Received in Service; Sickness or Hospitalization _____

_____

_____

Important Leaves or Furloughs _____

Discharged at or Separation _____

Name _____ Service Number _____ Job Classification _____

Enlisted or Inducted _____ Month _____ Day _____ Year _____ At Age _____

Branch of Service _____ Grade _____

Training Camps _____ Service Schools Attended _____

_____

Division _____ Regiment _____ Department or Ship _____ Dates _____

Company _____ Transferred _____

Promotion and Dates _____

_____

_____

Overseas Service _____ Departure Date _____ Port _____ Return Date _____ Port _____

_____

_____

Battles, Engagements, Skirmishes, Expeditions _____ Commanding Officers _____ Citations _____

_____

_____

Wounds Received in Service; Sickness or Hospitalization _____

_____

_____

Important Leaves or Furloughs _____

Discharged at or Separation _____

Notes: _____

_____

_____

Special Friends

Everyone has a special friend who sometimes seems like part of the family.
Certainly they make up some big parts of your life, so including them in
a family record book seems appropriate. Don't forget to include dates,
addresses and some of those things that make these people so special.

_____

_____

_____

_____

_____

_____

_____

_____

_____

_____

_____

_____

_____

_____

_____

_____

Special Friends

CONTINUED

Our Pets

The chances are millions to one that you have a pet elephant but more likely you have
a dog, cat, turtle or fish. Animals, like good friends, seem to become part of the family
and play a part in our daily lives. Because they are integrated into the 'family,'
remembering them will recall fond memories.

Owner _____ Pet's Name _____

Type of Pet _____ Dates of Ownership _____

_____

_____

Owner _____ Pet's Name _____

Type of Pet _____ Dates of Ownership _____

_____

_____

Owner _____ Pet's Name _____

Type of Pet _____ Dates of Ownership _____

_____

_____

Owner _____ Pet's Name _____

Type of Pet _____ Dates of Ownership _____

_____

_____

Owner _____ Pet's Name _____

Type of Pet _____ Dates of Ownership _____

_____

_____

Owner _____ Pet's Name _____

Type of Pet _____ Dates of Ownership _____

_____

_____

Owner _____ Pet's Name _____

Type of Pet _____ Dates of Ownership _____

_____

_____

Notes _____

_____

_____

_____

_____

_____

_____

_____

_____

_____

_____

_____

Our Pets

CONTINUED

Owner _____ Pet's Name _____

Type of Pet _____ Dates of Ownership _____

_____

_____

Owner _____ Pet's Name _____

Type of Pet _____ Dates of Ownership _____

_____

_____

Owner _____ Pet's Name _____

Type of Pet _____ Dates of Ownership _____

_____

_____

Owner _____ Pet's Name _____

Type of Pet _____ Dates of Ownership _____

_____

_____

Owner _____ Pet's Name _____

Type of Pet _____ Dates of Ownership _____

_____

_____

Owner _____ Pet's Name _____

Type of Pet _____ Dates of Ownership _____

_____

_____

Owner _____ Pet's Name _____

Type of Pet _____ Dates of Ownership _____

_____

_____

Owner _____ Pet's Name _____

Type of Pet _____ Dates of Ownership _____

_____

_____

Notes _____

_____

_____

_____

_____

_____

_____

_____

_____

_____

Automobiles

Americans have always been a people on the move and ever since Henry Ford started to mass produce cars they have been a part of almost every family's life. Every auto you have owned or will own has a special place in your life and remembering them will bring back lots of memories.

Owner _____   Make, Model, Year _____

Color _____   Dates of Ownership _____

Owner _____   Make, Model, Year _____

Color _____   Dates of Ownership _____

Owner _____   Make, Model, Year _____

Color _____   Dates of Ownership _____

Owner _____   Make, Model, Year _____

Color _____   Dates of Ownership _____

Owner _____   Make, Model, Year _____

Color _____   Dates of Ownership _____

Owner _____   Make, Model, Year _____

Color _____   Dates of Ownership _____

Owner _____   Make, Model, Year _____

Color _____   Dates of Ownership _____

Owner _____   Make, Model, Year _____

Color _____   Dates of Ownership _____

Owner _____   Make, Model, Year _____

Color _____   Dates of Ownership _____

Owner _____   Make, Model, Year _____

Color _____   Dates of Ownership _____

_____

_____

_____

_____

_____

_____

_____

_____

_____

_____

_____

_____

Favorite Things

His and Hers

Songs, Records, Books, Shows, Places, Recipes, etc.

_____

_____

_____

_____

_____

_____

_____

_____

_____

_____

_____

_____

_____

_____

_____

_____

Favorite Things

Children

Songs, Records, Stories, Toys, Places, Pastimes, Food etc.

Collections & Heirlooms

Include here special collections of various family members—what they are, when begun, how much collected, etc. List all heirlooms, including original owner and how items were passed from generation to generation. In short, record anything of interest to you that will also be of interest to others who read about your family.

Collections & Heirlooms

CONTINUED

Favorite Sports

Family or Individual's Name

Sport, Team, Club

Special Achievement

Family or Individual's Name

Sport, Team, Club

Special Achievement

Family or Individual's Name

Sport, Team, Club

Special Achievement

Family or Individual's Name

Sport, Team, Club

Special Achievement

Family or Individual's Name

Sport, Team, Club

Special Achievement

Family or Individual's Name _____

Sport, Team, Club _____

Special Achievement _____

Family or Individual's Name _____

Sport, Team, Club _____

Special Achievement _____

Family or Individual's Name _____

Sport, Team, Club _____

Special Achievement _____

Notes: _____

_____

_____

_____

_____

_____

_____

_____

_____

Favorite Sports

CONTINUED

Family or Individual's Name

Sport, Team, Club

Special Achievement

Family or Individual's Name

Sport, Team, Club

Special Achievement

Family or Individual's Name

Sport, Team, Club

Special Achievement

Family or Individual's Name

Sport, Team, Club

Special Achievement

Family or Individual's Name

Sport, Team, Club

Special Achievement

Family or Individual's Name _____

Sport, Team, Club _____

Special Achievement _____

Family or Individual's Name _____

Sport, Team, Club _____

Special Achievement _____

Family or Individual's Name _____

Sport, Team, Club _____

Special Achievement _____

Notes: _____

_____

_____

_____

_____

_____

_____

_____

_____

Favorite Hobbies

From woodcarving and quilt-making to rebuilding old cars and raising exotic plants,
many families have individuals who pursue a wide variety of interesting hobbies.
Here is a space to record those individuals and their pastimes and any fascinating pieces of
information about how they started and why, and whether anyone else followed in their footsteps.

Favorite Hobbies

CONTINUED

Vacations

Getting away from it all seems to keep us going through the rest of the year so entering some
of the places you go to, who was there, and what happened can help bring back some of that fun.
Some vacations are not so much where you went as what you did or who you met, so by
recording this you have the chance, in the future, to look back and smile or cry.

Reunions

Remembering who was there and at what occasion is a lot easier if you record it here.
In years to come this kind of information will conjure up the event all over again for you—
no matter if it was your Fifth High School Class Reunion or your Fiftieth Wedding Anniversary.

_____

_____

_____

_____

_____

_____

_____

_____

_____

_____

_____

_____

_____

_____

_____

_____

_____

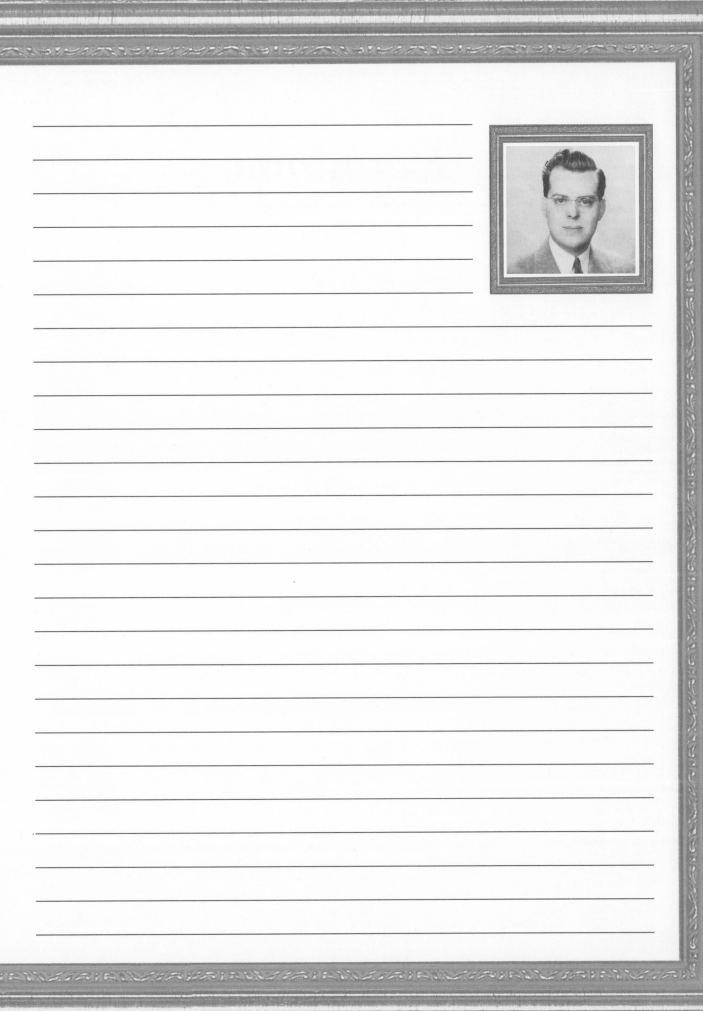

Reunions

CONTINUED

Traditions

_____

_____

_____

_____

_____

_____

_____

_____

_____

_____

_____

_____

_____

_____

_____

_____

_____

_____

_____

Events to Remember

Here you may record information about events (other than such things as
reunions, trips and club activities) that you may want to recall years from now.
Include family "firsts" and unique achievements—winning a special prize,
meeting a famed personality, witnessing an outstanding event.

_____

_____

_____

_____

_____

_____

_____

_____

_____

_____

_____

_____

_____

_____

_____

_____

Events to Remember

CONTINUED

Oral History

From survivors and participants in wars to migrations from other countries, each family has stories no one has ever written down. Here is a space to do so to record forever what would be lost if it remains "oral history."

_____

_____

_____

_____

_____

_____

_____

_____

_____

_____

_____

_____

_____

_____

_____

_____

_____

_____

Oral History

CONTINUED

Extraordinary Events

We have survived and overcome

Into each family comes those unforeseen events. Many have survived natural disasters (floods, tornadoes) and many times families were forced to move or were altered for the better as a result. Here is a space for you to record whatever you feel is appropriate in relation to your own family's experiences.

Illnesses

Name   Illness   Operation

Hospital   Doctor   Date

Name   Illness   Operation

Hospital   Doctor   Date

Name   Illness   Operation

Hospital   Doctor   Date

Name   Illness   Operation

Hospital   Doctor   Date

Name   Illness   Operation

Hospital   Doctor   Date

Name _____ Illness _____ Operation _____

Hospital _____ Doctor _____ Date _____

_____

Name _____ Illness _____ Operation _____

Hospital _____ Doctor _____ Date _____

_____

Name _____ Illness _____ Operation _____

Hospital _____ Doctor _____ Date _____

_____

Name _____ Illness _____ Operation _____

Hospital _____ Doctor _____ Date _____

_____

Name _____ Illness _____ Operation _____

Hospital _____ Doctor _____ Date _____

_____

Name _____ Illness _____ Operation _____

Hospital _____ Doctor _____ Date _____

_____

Vital Statistics

Space is provided on these pages for vital statistics. Fill in with as much detail as you care to note.

His

Weight _____

Hair Color _____

Eye Color _____

Suit Size _____

Shirt Size _____

Waist _____

Shoe Size _____

Hat Size _____

Ring Size _____

Other Sizes _____

_____

_____

Color Preference _____

_____

Toiletries Preferences _____

_____

_____

_____

Hers

Height _____

Weight _____

Hair Color _____

Eye Color _____

Blouse Size _____

Dress Size _____

Shoe Size _____

Ring Size _____

Other Sizes _____

_____

_____

_____

Color Preference _____

_____

_____

_____

Perfume and Toiletries Preferences _____

_____

_____

_____

Vital Statistics

Children

Name _____ Height _____ Weight _____

Hair Color _____ Eye Color _____ Suit Size _____ Shirt Size _____

Shoe Size _____ Hat Size _____ Ring Size _____ Other Size _____

Color Preference _____

Name _____ Height _____ Weight _____

Hair Color _____ Eye Color _____ Suit Size _____ Shirt Size _____

Shoe Size _____ Hat Size _____ Ring Size _____ Other Size _____

Color Preference _____

Name _____ Height _____ Weight _____

Hair Color _____ Eye Color _____ Suit Size _____ Shirt Size _____

Shoe Size _____ Hat Size _____ Ring Size _____ Other Size _____

Color Preference _____

Name _____ Height _____ Weight _____

Hair Color _____ Eye Color _____ Suit Size _____ Shirt Size _____

Shoe Size _____ Hat Size _____ Ring Size _____ Other Size _____

Color Preference _____

Name _____ Height _____ Weight _____

Hair Color _____ Eye Color _____ Suit Size _____ Shirt Size _____

Shoe Size _____ Hat Size _____ Ring Size _____ Other Size _____

Color Preference _____

Name _____ Height _____ Weight _____

Hair Color _____ Eye Color _____ Suit Size _____ Shirt Size _____

Shoe Size _____ Hat Size _____ Ring Size _____ Other Size _____

Color Preference _____

Name _____ Height _____ Weight _____

Hair Color _____ Eye Color _____ Suit Size _____ Shirt Size _____

Shoe Size _____ Hat Size _____ Ring Size _____ Other Size _____

Color Preference _____

Name _____ Height _____ Weight _____

Hair Color _____ Eye Color _____ Suit Size _____ Shirt Size _____

Shoe Size _____ Hat Size _____ Ring Size _____ Other Size _____

Color Preference _____

Name _____ Height _____ Weight _____

Hair Color _____ Eye Color _____ Suit Size _____ Shirt Size _____

Shoe Size _____ Hat Size _____ Ring Size _____ Other Size _____

Color Preference _____

Photographs

Pictures do their own story telling and in years to come a lot can be learned from this kind of record. You and future generations will be able to look back and see a member of the family in his or her own time and place. (You may also want to include favorite clippings, mementos, or documents.)

Photographs

Genealogy Research

Helpful Hints &
Do's and Don'ts in Tracing

All of us know something about our living relatives. We enjoy telling stories about their achievements and exploits, and we certainly have a fondness for the endearing characters that are in most families. Yet our knowledge of our families often does not go beyond those members we actually know. Few of us have been lucky enough to have known our great-grandparents for example. This shows us that one of the most common ways of learning about ourselves is by word of mouth; the so-called oral tradition. Thus, if you want to begin finding out more about your family the place to start is with your relatives. Ask them if they can provide you with birth dates, places of residence and dates of death of those whom you do not know, such as your great-grandparents. Do this as far as it is possible to trace them. Also, check to see if there are any relatives who have previously done genealogical research that might aid in your search. Once you have reached this point you will discover the great treasures of information available in family bibles, picture, albums, old letters, diaries and account books. Your ancestors often kept better records than you think!

If you have access to a computer, search the Internet for surnames you have found (mother's maiden name, grandmother's maiden name, etc.)

You might discover some useful information or even come across others who are doing research on the same lines of genealogy as you. There are many websites and message boards devoted entirely to genealogy. Check them out, look for surnames, get what help you can from them.

Once you have names, dates and places you can consult town records. Securing birth certificates, marriage licenses, death certificates, wills and land deeds will give you additional names you will want and need. Don't be disappointed if some of these public records are not available. You can always check your public library. Some of the subjects you can look up at the library are clans, deeds, epitaphs, estates, marriage licenses, nobility, parish registers, peerage and precedence. Also don't forget to ask the librarian for additional sources of genealogical information. If the books listed in the card catalogue are not in the stacks, your librarian can easily send for them.

Another place to check is your state genealogical association or historical society. Each state has its own organization with qualified people who can be very helpful in local matters. These associations also often publish their own periodicals that you might like to look into. The Daughters of the American Revolution in your area may also be able to furnish you with further information. Sometimes they too publish interesting pamphlets on the subject.

The next step in your search is to contact the National Archives (www.archives.gov), which is the central United States depository for records, located in Washington, D.C., to find out which of their eleven regional branches is nearest you. The National Archives contain many different kinds of records which will be helpful to you. The Census Records, from 1790 to date, are kept here. They give information such as the name of each family member, age, occupation and place of birth. Also available are records of military service, pensions and land grants. Since we are a nation of immigrants you may find here the names of the first members of your family who came to America, as well as the name of the ship that brought them, the date of arrival, the port of entry and the date of naturalization. For other such information one should consult the United States Immigration and Naturalization office.

For the majority of us our families have only lived in America for three or four generations. It was about this time that the mass immigrations from other countries to the United States began. Thus far, all of the research information has concentrated on relatives who lived in America. There is no need to stop researching at this point however, because there are sources available to help you trace your ancestors to the countries that they originally came from. The library of the Church of Jesus Christ of Latter-Day Saints in Salt Lake City contains the largest collection of genealogical information dat-

ing from 1538 to 1805. It contains records from the national and local archives, courthouses, cemeteries, churches and a variety of other places where records were kept, about people all over the world. Some 40 countries are represented in this collection of genealogical data. This enormous library has branches around the world and since they require that you do your own research you can contact them at www.familysearch.org for more information. The library's researchers are continually making copies of genealogical records throughout the world to further expand the collection.

For the most part, at this point your have completed all of the research that can be done in America and it is time to write away to foreign countries to get additional information. To find out where and to whom to write you should contact the consulate of the country to which you are writing. Once the consulate has sent you the correct address and the name of the person to whom you should write, do not hesitate because you don't speak the language; the agency will get someone to translate your letter for them. It is very important to include as much pertinent information as you have. Names, dates, places of residence are especially necessary. One thing you must consider is that often when people arrived in America from other countries their names were misspelled or arbitrarily anglicized and therefore you must know what their name was originally before you make any inquiries.

The charts that appear in this book go back five generations, about 150 years. These five generations represent about 124 people in a direct line descendancy.

Helpful Resources

Addresses

Family Search
(formerly Genealogical Society of Utah)
The Church of Jesus Christ
of Latter-Day Saints
50 E. North Temple Street
Salt Lake City, Utah 84150
Ph: 1-801-240-1000
www.familysearch.org

The National Archives and
Records Administration
8601 Adelphi Road
College Park, MD 20740-6001
Ph: 1-866-272-6272
www.archives.gov

Board for the Certification
of Genealogists
P.O. Box 14291
Washington, D.C. 20044
www.bcgcertification.org

Publications

Family Chronicle Magazine
(**www.familychronicle.com**)

Family Tree Magazine
(**www.familytreemagazine.com**)

Everton's Family History Magazine
(**www.legacyfamilytree.com**)

Eastman's Online Genealogy Newsletter
(**www.eogn.com**)

Heritage Quest
(**https://hqrl.com**)

Ancestor News
(**www.ancestornews.com**)

Your Genealogy Today
(**www.yourgenealogytoday.com**)

Websites

23andme.com (DNA testing)

www.jewishgen.org
(Guide, information, websites, tips)

www.cyndislist.com
(Guide, information, websites, tips)

www.ancestry.com (Genealogy)

www.rootsweb.com (Genealogy)

www.onegreatfamily.com (Genealogy)

www.genealogytoday.com (Genealogy)

www.genealogytoday.com/ca
(Genealogy, Canadian)

www.ellisisland.org (Ellis Island)

www.libertyellisfoundation.org
(Passenger search and
US Immigration data search)

www.usgenweb.org
(USGenWeb Project)

www.rootsweb.com/~canwgw/
Canada GenWeb Project)

www.loc.gov/rr/genealogy
(Library of Congress)

www.acgs.org
(American-Canadian\Genealogical
Society)

www.collectionscanada.ca
(Library and Archives Canada)

www.houseofnames.com

www.heritagebooks.com

http://newspaperarchive.com
(Searchable newspapers dating
back to 1748)

Bookstores which specialize in genealogical material

Genealogical Publishing Co., Inc.
1001 N. Calvert Street
Baltimore, MD 21202-3897
Ph: 1-410-837-8271
Fax: 1-410-752-8492
Orders: sales@genealogical.com
www.genealogical.com

Higginson Book Company
P.O. Box 778
10 Colonial Road
Suite 5-6
Salem, MA 01970
Ph: 1-978-745-7170
Fax: 1-978-745-8025
higginsonbookscompany@gmail.com

Willow Bend Books
A Division of Heritage Books, Inc.
65 E. Main Street
Westminster, MD 21157
Ph: 1-800-876-6103
Fax: 1-410-871-2674
Contact: info@heritagebooks.com
www.heritagebooks.com

Bibliography

American Genealogical Research Institute. How to Trace Your Family Tree. Dolphin Books.

Bennett, Archibald F. Finding Your Forefathers in America. Salt Lake City, Bookcraft Co., 1957.

Bidlack, Russell Eugene. First Steps in Climbing the Family Tree. Detroit Society for Genealogical Research, 1966.

Doane, Gilbert H. Searching for Your Ancestors. New York, Bantam Books, Inc., 1974.

Everton, George B. The Handbook for Genealogist. Logan, Utah, Everton Publishers, 1962.

Greenwood, Val D. The Researcher's Guide to American Genealogy. Genealogical Publishing Co., 1973.

Iredale, David. Discovering Your Family Tree. Shire Publications.

National Genealogical Society. Special Publications: No. 17, Genealogy, Handmaid of History.
(A list can be obtained of other articles from the Society, 1921 Sunderland Place, N.W., Washington, D.C. 20036)

Rottenberg, Dan. Finding Our Fathers. New York, Random House, 1977.

Williams, Ethel W. Know Your Ancestors. Rutland, Vt., C.E. Tuttle Co., 1964.